FREAKY PHENOMENA

LIFE AFTER DEATH

FREAKY PHENOMENA

The Series

CONSCIOUSNESS
FAITH
HEALING
LIFE AFTER DEATH
MYSTERIOUS PLACES
PERSONALITY
PSYCHIC ABILITIES
THE SENSES

FREAKY PHENOMENA

LIFE AFTER DEATH

Don Rauf

Foreword by Joe Nickell, Senior Research Fellow, Committee for Skeptical Inquiry

MASON CREST

Mason Crest
450 Parkway Drive, Suite D Broomall, PA 19008
www.masoncrest.com

Printed in the United States of America

First printing
9 8 7 6 5 4 3 2 1

Series ISBN: 978-1-4222-3772-4
Hardcover ISBN: 978-1-4222-3776-2
ebook ISBN: 978-1-4222-8010-2

Cataloging-in-Publication Data is available on file at the Library of Congress.

Developed and Produced by Print Matters Productions, Inc. (www.printmattersinc.com)
Cover and Interior Design by: Bill Madrid, Madrid Design
Composition by Carling Design

Picture credits: 9, pxl.store/Shutterstock; 10, Bliznetsov/iStock; 12, Salvador Aznar/Shutterstock; 12, Kerrie Jones/Shutterstock; 12, Pecold/Shutterstock; 14, Georgios Kollidas/Shutterstock; 15, Anton_Ivanov/Shutterstock; 16, Balate Dorin/Shutterstock; 18, sdominick/iStock; 20, andriano.cz/Shutterstock; 23, Helga Esteb/Shutterstock; 24, vale_t/iStock; 26, Eagle9/Shutterstock; 27, Janusz Pienkowski/Shutterstock; 28, wavebreakmedia/Shutterstock; 30, HrGa2112/iStock; 32, By unidentified photographer via Wikimedia Commons; 34, By User:Doron via Wikimedia Commons; 35, Bill Perry/Shutterstock; 36, KatarzyanBialasiewicz/iStock; 38, duncan1890/iStock; 40, Renphoto/iStock; 42, nutech21/Shutterstock

Cover: sdominick/iStock

38179000316149
1/19

CONTENTS

KEY ICONS TO LOOK FOR:

Words to understand: These words with their easy-to-understand definitions will increase the reader's understanding of the text while building vocabulary skills.

Sidebars: This boxed material within the main text allows readers to build knowledge, gain insights, explore possibilities, and broaden their perspectives by weaving together additional information to provide realistic and holistic perspectives.

Educational Videos: Readers can view videos by scanning our QR codes, providing them with additional educational content to supplement the text. Examples include news coverage, moments in history, speeches, iconic sports moments and much more!

Series glossary of key terms: This back-of-the book glossary contains terminology used throughout this series. Words found here increase the reader's ability to read and comprehend higher-level books and articles in this field.

Advice From a Full-Time Professional Investigator of Strange Mysteries

I wish I'd had books like this when I was young. Like other boys and girls, I was intrigued by ghosts, monsters, and other freaky things. I grew up to become a stage magician and private detective, as well as (among other things) a literary and folklore scholar and a forensic-science writer. By 1995, I was using my varied background as the world's only full-time professional investigator of strange mysteries.

As I travel around the world, lured by its enigmas, I avoid both uncritical belief and outright dismissal. I insist mysteries should be *investigated* with the intent of solving them. That requires *critical thinking*, which begins by asking useful questions. I share three such questions here, applied to brief cases from my own files:

Is a particular story really true?

Consider Louisiana's Myrtles Plantation, supposedly haunted by the ghost of a murderous slave, Chloe. We are told that, as revenge against a cruel master, she poisoned three members of his family. Phenomena that ghost hunters attributed to her spirit included a mysteriously swinging door and unexplained banging noises.

The Discovery TV Channel arranged for me to spend a night there alone. I learned from the local historical society that Chloe never existed and her three alleged victims actually died in a yellow fever epidemic. I prowled the house, discovering that the spooky door was simply hung off center, and that banging noises were easily explained by a loose shutter.

Does a claim involve unnecessary assumptions?

In Flatwoods, WV, in 1952, some boys saw a fiery UFO streak across the evening sky and apparently land on a hill. They went looking for it, joined by others. A flashlight soon revealed a tall creature with shining eyes and a face shaped like the ace of spades. Suddenly, it swooped at them with "terrible claws," making a high-pitched hissing sound. The witnesses fled for their lives.

Half a century later, I talked with elderly residents, examined old newspaper accounts, and did other research. I learned the UFO had been a meteor. Descriptions of the creature almost perfectly matched a barn owl—seemingly tall because it had perched on a tree limb. In contrast, numerous incredible assumptions would be required to argue for a flying saucer and an alien being.

Is the proof as great as the claim?

A Canadian woman sometimes exhibited the crucifixion wounds of Jesus—allegedly produced supernaturally. In 2002, I watched blood stream from her hands and feet and from tiny scalp wounds like those from a crown of thorns.

However, because her wounds were already bleeding, they could have been self-inflicted. The lance wound that pierced Jesus' side was absent, and the supposed nail wounds did not pass through the hands and feet, being only on one side of each. Getting a closer look, I saw that one hand wound was only a small slit, not a large puncture wound. Therefore, this extraordinary claim lacked the extraordinary proof required.

These three questions should prove helpful in approaching claims and tales in Freaky Phenomena. I view the progress of science as a continuing series of solved mysteries. Perhaps you too might consider a career as a science detective. You can get started right here.

Joe Nickell

Senior Research Fellow, Committee for Skeptical Inquiry

Amherst, NY

GONE BUT NOT FORGOTTEN

Throughout history, people have believed that there is life beyond this one on Earth. Major religions, such as Christianity and Islam, support the concept. In Judaism, the sacred book the Torah speaks of a life to follow this one.

Just as some people believe that our spirits live on after we die, many also believe that the dead can somehow contact the living—appearing as ghosts or communicating through mediums. Often the stories of loved ones getting in touch after death are much more subtle—people claim to smell their scent, sense their presence, feel their touch, or hear their voice. The deceased might even appear in a dream. Scientists say this is all a trick of the mind—a coping mechanism to relieve grief in times of sorrow.

Despite this logical explanation, people still swear they have experienced a visit from a loved one who has died. On July 31, 2014, a woman in Northern Ireland said that her husband came home from his work after midnight and placed his car keys on the bedroom cabinet. He got into bed, but at 3:00 a.m. he and his wife were woken up when the keys flew across the room and clattered to the floor. Neither could explain it, but the husband appeared to be especially bothered. The couple was driving to the airport the next day, when the husband said to his wife, "We are going to be in a car crash today." The wife laughed at him and told him not to worry.

They made it to the airport safely and took off. When they arrived in London, they were picked up by a friend. The wife got in the back in the middle seat and did not put on her seat belt. The husband insisted, so she finally buckled up. Five minutes later, they were slammed by another car. The couple were seriously injured.

After the accident, the astonished wife asked her husband how he knew this would hap-

The historic landmark Chelsea Hotel in New York City is rumored to be haunted by former residents who died there.

pen. He said that he had seen his dead cousin Sean throw the keys. His dead grandmother also had appeared in the bedroom. They had both cautioned him not to go to London or harm would come his way. He went despite the eerie warning because he wanted to make sure his wife would be safe. If he hadn't gone, she would not have buckled up.

This eerie tale is typical of many supposed accounts of life after death. In this book we explore different types of afterlife experiences, including near-death experiences and reincarnation, and how science explains them.

CHAPTER 1

GHOSTS

Ghost sightings are
most often reported
around the place where
the person died.

Do you believe in ghosts? If you answer yes, you are not alone. A 2013 Harris Poll found that 40 percent of Americans think that ghosts are real. Ghosts are spirits or **apparitions** of a dead person (or animal). They appear in the world of the living. Typically, they show themselves as some sort of see-through figure, or they are invisible but causing a physical disturbance—a bump in the night or furniture sliding across the floor. Ghosts may be the most popular sign that there is some form of **afterlife**. Ancient Egyptians mentioned these spirits, as did the Chinese. In 786, Chinese Emperor Hsuan ordered his minister Tu-Po killed. Before he died, Tu-Po warned the emperor that he would come back to haunt him. In recounting the story, Chinese philosopher Mo Tzu wrote that three years after Tu-Po was executed, "Hsuan was killed with an arrow fired by an apparition resembling Tu-Po in front of an assembly of feudal lords."

Ghosts are often believed to be troubled or tormented souls that haunt the sites where they died. Often, these spirits suffered some sort of traumatic death on earth—an accident, a murder, a suicide. A common belief is that ghosts are spirits of people who have died too soon and are taking care of unfinished business. Believers say that some ghosts who died unfairly are looking for vengeance or justice. There are thousands of haunted locations—houses, castles, hotels, saloons, stores—around the globe, but a ghost also may attach itself to an object—a doll or jewelry. In addition, there have

Words to Understand

Afterlife: Life after death.

Apparition: A ghost or ghostlike image of a person.

Audible: Loud enough to be heard.

Hallucinate: To experience a perception of something that seems real but is not actually present.

Visage: Appearance.

The Emily Morgan Hotel in San Antonio, Lafitte's Blacksmith Shop in New Orleans, and Houska Castle near Prague in the Czech Republic are some of the most frequently named places for ghost sightings in the world.

been sightings of ghost ships—entire vessels that have disappeared ages ago that reappear as phantom images.

Some believe that spirits are a residual energy of a traumatic event that is somehow etched in the fabric of time. The ghosts seem to appear on the anniversary of the event. Since Eastern Airlines Flight 401 fell from the sky into the Everglades in Florida in 1972, the pilot and flight engineer have supposedly returned to haunt other Eastern Airlines flights, sometimes warning the crew of danger. In one instance, a flight attendant said she saw the deceased engineer's face in a galley oven. She heard a voice say, "Watch out for fire on this airplane." During the flight, the plane developed serious engine trouble and had to make an emergency landing.

Scientific Take: Unseen Forces Explained

Scientists have numerous explanations for what may cause people to perceive ghostly appearances. Canadian neuroscientist Michael Persinger believes that unseen electromagnetic fields can cause a subconscious feeling that there is a presence in a room. Infrasound, noises that are at the lower limit of **audibility**, can create a similar sensation in addition to feelings of panic and disorientation. Shawn Rogers, a professor at Clarkson University in Potsdam, NY, believes that many haunted houses have molds that can be toxic and trigger strange mental reactions, such as **hallucinating**. People may also hallucinate from drug or alcohol use, lack of sleep, or mental problems. Because so many people believe in ghosts, they may have a desire to interpret explainable phenomena as being otherworldly. In other words, they want so badly to see a ghost that they think they do. Remember, though, chances are a flickering light is just a momentary disruption in electricity, not a sign from the dead.

Anniversary Ghosts

Many ghosts appear only on the anniversary of their death. The Tower of London is a major site for such apparitions. Lady Jane Grey, who was an heir to the English throne and was beheaded on February 12, 1554, when she was about 16 years old, is said to return every year on that date, floating on a cloud of mist. King Henry VI was stabbed to death as he knelt praying in Wakefield Tower, part of the Tower of London complex. Every anniversary of his death, his ghost is said to pace around the exact spot where he met his grisly end, and then disappear at precisely midnight. The Countess of Salisbury, Margaret Pole, had one of the more gruesome, botched deaths at the Tower of London. After three swings of the axe, she did not die, but broke free of captors and ran away screaming. She was dragged back to the chopping block. A fourth swing of the axe did not finish her off—she was left with a deep wound in her neck and choking on her own blood. The fifth and final blow finally took off her head. On the anniversary of her execution, witnesses have seen a woman's apparition running about the tower yard and have heard ghostly screams. Ann Boleyn, the second wife of King Henry the VIII, gives Margaret Pole competition—she's been spotted roaming the grounds with her severed head tucked under her arm.

Some ghost stories have become the stuff of legend. In Jamestown, NC, people have for decades reported seeing a young woman in white hitchhiking along the road by a bridge, now called Lydia's Bridge. She flags down a car, gets in, and directs the driver to take her to an address. When the driver stops to let her out, she has disappeared. Lydia died in a car wreck returning from a party, and some say she is still trying to find her way home. The **visage** of a "white lady" is a commonly reported form of ghost.

More interesting ghost sightings caught on tape.

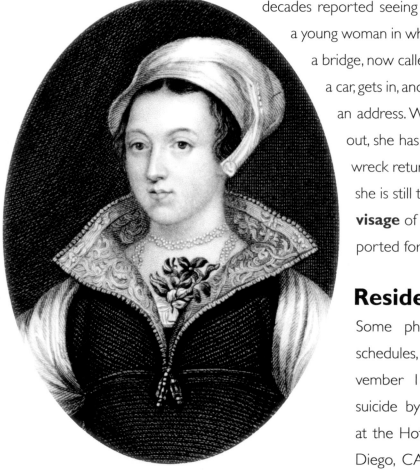

Lady Jane Grey is said to appear floating on a cloud of mist every year on the anniversary of her execution.

Resident Ghosts

Some phantoms have more irregular schedules, appearing at odd times. In November 1892, Kate Morgan committed suicide by shooting herself in the head at the Hotel del Coronado south of San Diego, CA. On occasion, an image of a woman in Victorian garb is seen floating through the halls—also, people claim to see lights flicker on and off and hear odd noises. President Abraham Lincoln's ghost has supposedly been seen on several occasions at the White House. Winston Churchill, who was an overnight guest at the White House at the time, reportedly met the ghost of Lincoln after emerging naked from the bathtub. Without a stitch on, Churchill confronted Lincoln standing near the fireplace. He said, "Good evening, Mr. President. You seem to have me at a disadvantage." Lincoln smiled softly and disappeared. In Alcatraz Prison, visitors swear they hear the ghost of gangster Al Capone playing one of his favorite instruments—the banjo. Almost anywhere people have died, the living see ghosts—from dead climbers begging

Maddam Tussaud's Wax Museum in San Francisco recreated the scene of Al Capone playing his favorite instrument in his Alcatraz cell.

for food atop Mount Everest to those who committed suicide in the Aokigahara Forest at the foot of Mount Fuji in Japan.

The Brown Lady of Raynham Hall is one of the most famous ghosts ever because she was apparently captured in a photo published on December 16, 1936, in *Country Life*. In the shot, she is dressed in brown floating down the staircase. Several have seen the specter of a woman wandering the manor in Norfolk, England. She is suspected to be Lady Dorothy Townshend who was imprisoned in the manor by her husband after she had an affair. Legend says she lived out her life there, never allowed to see anyone, not even her children. The photo itself has been proven the work of trick photography.

Sometimes a ghost might make itself known through sound rather than sight. In a *Twilight Zone* episode a boy can communicate with his dead grandmother over a toy telephone. Horror fiction

Ghost Forms
People tend to see ghosts in several forms. Here are a few popular presentations:

• **Spirit orbs.** Paranormal believers say these images of ghostly balls that appear in photos and videos represent energy patterns of ghosts.

• **Apparitions.** These are the most common way that people envision ghosts. Often a see-through figure of a person, a specter or phantom of a person once living.

• **Poltergeists.** From the German for "noisy spirits," these ghosts cause actual physical disturbances—they can make furniture move, doors knock, lamps fly, and lights flicker. They may communicate audibly or in writing.

• **Shadow people/ghosts.** Spirits that appear as dark shadows and are often thought to be evil. Some call them *djinns* (genies), and they can come as black mists or black ectoplasms.

writer Dean Koontz said that something similar happened to him in real life. He got a call on September 20, 1988. A faraway voice on the other end said four times "Please, be careful" and then disappeared. He thought the voice sounded like his mother who had been dead for 20 years. Two days after the call, Koontz went to a mental health facility to visit his ill father, who came at him with a knife and tried to kill him—the ghostly voice of his mother replayed in the writer's mind.

Loved Ones Return

The most common ghost sightings are of a loved one. A study from the University of Gothenburg in Sweden found that 8 out of 10 elderly people have had some sort of vision or contact from a loved one who had passed away. In 2002, a German woman told researchers that she regularly saw her daughter who died of a heroin overdose. At times, she would hear her say, "Mama! Mama!" and "It's so cold!" Some say they have even had a conversation with a ghost of a person they have lost. Scientists believe these to be hallucinations produced when people are emotionally distraught over the loss of a loved one. The grieving mind produces a vision of a ghost that in some way may help relieve the pain.

Famous Ghost Ships

In the ghostly realm, one of the more common phenomena is the mysterious reappearance of ships that have vanished. Sometimes the actual ships are found but mysteriously sailing without a crew. Here are a few of the most famous so-called ghost ships:

The Flying Dutchman. For centuries, sailors have spied a ghostly schooner with its sails up (sometimes in tatters) drifting out of the dark or fog and then disappearing. In 1942, Nazi admiral Karl Dönitz swore that he spied the *Dutchman*.

SS Baychimo. On October 1, 1931, this 1,322-ton, steam-powered vessel was transporting a cargo of furs from Alaska to Vancouver in British Columbia. The boat got caught in a fierce storm and had to be abandoned. The crew made attempts to reclaim the ship, but in the end they took what cargo they could and then let the damaged vessel sail free. For decades afterward, sightings of the ship were reported although it disappeared or eluded anyone trying to catch up to it. In 1962 some Inuit people claimed to have seen it drifting along the coastline. In 1969, it was spotted several more times.

Mary Celeste. This American merchant brigantine was discovered adrift and deserted in the Atlantic Ocean, off the Azores Islands, on December 5, 1872. The captain and his crew had completely disappeared. The mystery has never been solved.

CHAPTER 2

NEAR-DEATH EXPERIENCE

People's accounts of near-death experiences tend to follow a similar pattern involving tunnels, bright lights, and the sensation of rising out of your body and looking down at it.

P eople who have come close to death believe they have had a glimpse of what the afterlife may be like. Near-death experiences (sometimes shortened to NDEs) can produce sensations that may seem almost supernatural. The concept goes back hundreds of years. The journal *Resuscitation* published an account of what may be the oldest known medical description of an NDE, written by an 18th-century French military doctor.

Many who are thought to have clinically died but came back to life experience a sensation of levitation or detachment from the body. When Jazmyne Cidavia-DeRepentigny of Hull, GA, "died" on the operating table during surgery in late 1979, she said she had an **out-of-body experience**. She felt as though she were floating over her body and could see all that was being done. She observed that she had stopped breathing although medical staff were unaware. To get their attention, she tried to make her arm move on her physical body, but she could not at first. She struggled and finally her arm did move. When doctors noticed, she was given the oxygen she needed. She described the experience as feeling a pull between two worlds—a desire to stay on earth but also a longing to become her spirit self and go into the light.

Words to Understand

Anoxia: An absence of oxygen.

Déjà vu: A sensation of experiencing something that has happened before when experienced for the first time.

Endorphins: Hormones secreted by the brain that reduce pain and can produce a feeling of euphoria.

Euphoria: An intense state of happiness; elation.

Out-of-body experience: A sensation of being outside one's body, floating above and observing events, often when unconscious or clinically dead.

An out-of-body experience typically involves the feeling of floating outside one's body.

Others who have momentarily died have also referred to this light, which they often describe as full of warmth and love. Many who have had NDEs describe passing through a tunnel, being greeted by dead relatives and friends, or meeting a loving being, which they interpret as God. Consistently, NDEs seem to bring an overall feeling of peace and **euphoria**.

A View from Above

Those seeking to prove that NDE is real look for accounts from those who have "died" that show they have seen or heard something that they otherwise could not have known. For example, a migrant worker known only as "Maria" had a heart attack in a Seattle hospital in April of 1976. Her heart stopped for several minutes. When she experienced the sensation of floating above her body, she saw a tennis shoe on a window ledge. When she was revived, she described the shoe in great detail—dark blue with a scuffmark by the toe and lace going under the heel, and hospital staff confirmed her description. The story is often repeated, but it is difficult to verify who Maria exactly was.

In the book *Near-Death Experiences: Understanding Visions of the Afterlife*, authors John Martin Fischer and Benjamin Mitchell-Yellin recount the story of a man who was having a heart attack and undergoing CPR (cardiopulmonary resuscitation). He later described feeling himself rise out of his body and seeing a nurse put his dentures in a drawer. When he was revived, he was able to tell the medical staff exactly where his dentures were.

In 1991, an American singer/songwriter named Pam Reynolds, 35, had to have surgery for a brain aneurysm. Her heart was stopped and her brain was put into an inactive state—she later described having felt herself rise out of her body and was able to accurately recount snatches of conversation and other details from the operating room. Although her ears were covered by special headphones that emitted loud clicks, she might have heard the conversation.

In her book *Near Death Experiences, the Rest of the Story: What They Teach Us About Living and Dying* and *Our True Purpose*, author P. M. H. Atwater recounts the story of a man from Portland, OR, whose car skidded on black ice and crashed into a tree. The man recalled floating up above the accident scene and looking down to see his body, an arm missing, the car a wreck, and lots of blood. His spirit thought he could live if he got help. He saw a house nearby, a light on in the second story. He floated to the window and started jumping up and down and screaming repeatedly as loudly as he could "There's been an accident! Call the police!" A person inside later told police that he had seen some type of "jumping fog" outside and had heard the message that there had been an accident and to call the police.

Dr. George Rodonaia, a scientist from the Soviet Union, was run over by a car in 1976 and declared dead at the hospital. His spirit was drawn to the newborn section where he saw that a friend's wife had given birth to a daughter. Noticing that the baby was crying a lot, he examined the X-ray during his out-of-body experience. Rodonaia saw the baby's hip had been broken after birth—somehow he knew that the nurse had dropped the baby. When Rodoaia was revived, he told the story to medical staff. They verified his vision. When confronted with the details, the nurse confirmed the story and was fired.

The Scientific Take: They're Not Dead Yet

In the comedy movie *Monty Python and the Holy Grail,* a man goes about collecting the dead plague victims. One man being carted away complains that he's "not dead yet!" This is essentially the way scientists explain near-death experiences. What people interpret as near-death are actually sensations that a living person can have within the brain. The body and brain are responding to the trauma; the visions may be triggered by a lack of oxygen and stress to the brain. One theory is that the brain still registers activity when one is unconscious and that the memories re-emerge later. *Near Death Experiences, the Rest of the Story* describes the work of Kevin Nelson, a practicing neurologist who has studied NDEs. His data show that real physical experiences could be the cause of what is interpreted as an NDE; these include drifting in and out of consciousness and changes in blood flow during a health crisis. It's possible that the visions are along the lines of a hallucination. **Endorphins** can be released under stress creating euphoria. Lack of oxygen (**anoxia**) confuses the brain and how it perceives things. Anoxia may explain why so many people describe a tunnel with light at the end. In her book *Dying to Live*, British psychologist Susan Blackmore says that temporal lobe seizures may cause a person to review their life. She adds that accurate perceptions during NDE may be due to prior knowledge, fantasy, lucky guesses, and the remaining functioning senses—hearing and touch.

Stories of near-death experiences.

Famous Glimpses of the Great Beyond

The Greek philosopher Plato wrote of an NDE, in his dialogue the Republic. He recounted the story of Er, a soldier who awoke after being dead for 12 days to share his account of the journey to the afterlife. Thomas Edison once wrote that when a person dies a swarm of charged energies exits the body and goes into space and enters another cycle of life.

The author Ernest Hemingway wrote of his near-death experience in World War I: "A big Austrian trench mortar bomb, of the type that used to be called ash cans, exploded in the darkness. I died then. I felt my soul or something coming right out of my body, like you'd pull a silk handkerchief out of a pocket by one corner. It flew around and then came back and went in again and I wasn't dead anymore."

After comedian Tracy Morgan was in a devastating multicar crash in 2014, he was in a coma. During that time, he said he met God, who told him: "Your room ain't ready. I still got something for you to do." Morgan has recovered and continues to perform.

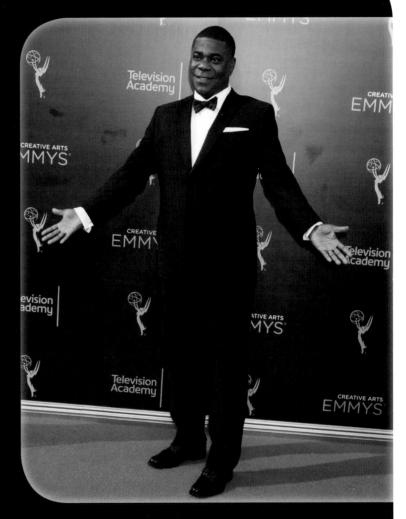

Comedian Tracy Morgan described a near-death experience after nearly dying in a car accident.

CHAPTER 3

REINCARNATION

Buddhists, such as these monks at a temple complex in China, believe that when a person dies, they are reborn or reincarnated.

A number of Asian religions, including Hinduism, Buddhism, Taoism, and Sikhism, believe that humans can be reborn. According to these religions, our **immortal** souls can come back in different incarnations. When a person dies, the soul is reborn into a new body. The notion of reincarnation is linked to the idea of **karma**. In these Eastern religions, karma is the sum of a person's actions in this and all previous lives. Karma decides their fate in future incarnations. Simply put, we keep coming back to live new lives to improve on the mistakes we made in former lives. Souls are on a mission to evolve. The goal is to reach a state of perfect **enlightenment** at which point reincarnation is no longer necessary. Each time a soul comes back it is striving for greater levels of love, goodness, and wisdom. For instance, a person might come back as a different sex in order to appreciate the full spectrum of life.

Reincarnation has its downside, too. If you do bad deeds in this life you could be reborn into a lower life form—such as a pig or a fly. Some reincarnation believers think that people meet others from their past lives as well, from lovers to enemies. Chance meetings aren't always so chance in this scheme—the fates are giving people another opportunity to work things out. Reincarnation believers say the eyes are the gateway to the soul and sometimes looking into another person's eyes will reveal a past connection. Talents and skills also may carry over from one life to the next. Have a seemingly born talent to play music? You may have been a musician in a previous life. Some even think pets rein-

Words to Understand

Immortal: Living forever.

Enlightenment: Awareness that brings change.

Karma: A Buddhist belief that whatever one does comes back—a person's actions can determine his or her reincarnation.

Phobia: Extreme irrational fear.

The Reincarnated Religious Leader

The Dalai Lama is the spiritual head of Tibetan Buddhism and for centuries the position has been filled through reincarnation. The current Dalai Lama is the reincarnation of the previous one who died. When a Dalai Lama passes, Buddhist high religious leaders meditate beside a lake and experience visions and dreams that guide their search. The new Dalai Lama is always a child. To test if he is the one, items from the previous Dalai Lama are placed before him, and he is asked to choose which were his. Other senior lamas are also reincarnated and chosen in this way. In 2009, a nine-year-old Minnesota boy who enjoyed soccer, Pokémon, and swimming was identified as the reincarnation of a senior lama.

The Dalai Lama is the spiritual leader of Tibetan Buddhism.

carnate. If you do believe in reincarnation, you are not alone: a 2011 poll from the Roper Center found that one in five Americans believe in reincarnation.

Learn about the growing belief in reincarnation in the United States.

Past Life Regression

Past life regression, a type of therapy, uses hypnosis so patients can access memories of their past lives with a goal of having a spiritual awakening or sorting out psychological problems in their current life. Dr. Brian Weiss, of Miami, FL, uses this technique—he leads patients back to their earliest memories of childhood and then takes them back further into previous lives, when experiences shaped current fears and **phobias**. Understanding the source of these fears is thought to help some people free themselves of the fear.

Dr. Weiss had one patient, Jodi, who had an intense fear of dolls since childhood. She never wanted to hold a doll when she was little, and she later refused to buy her own children any dolls. Under hypnosis, Jodi gained memories of a past life in which she died in an accident and worried about protecting her children. Dr. Weiss believes that dolls represented Jodi's children from the prior life, and she maintained an intense worry about protecting them.

Famous Believers

Many Western thinkers and leaders have expressed a belief in reincarnation in their writings. Among these are Socrates, Pythagoras, Plato, Dante, Ralph Waldo Emerson, Henry David Thoreau, Goethe, Albert Schweitzer, and George Patton. Here are a few thoughts on reincarnation from famous figures:

Johann Wolfgang von Goethe (German author): "I am certain I have been here as I am now a thousand times before, and I hope to return a thousand times."

Henry Ford (American industrialist): "I adopted the theory of reincarnation when I was 26 ... Work is futile if we cannot utilize the experience we collect in one life in the next. When I discovered reincarnation, it was as if I had found a universal plan ... Time was no longer limited. I was no longer a slave to the hands of the clock ... Genius is experience ... It is the fruit of long experience in many lives ... The discovery of reincarnation put my mind at ease."

John Masefield (English poet): "I hold that when a person dies his soul returns again to earth; arrayed in some new flesh-disguise another mother gives him birth. With sturdier limbs and brighter brain the old soul takes the road again."

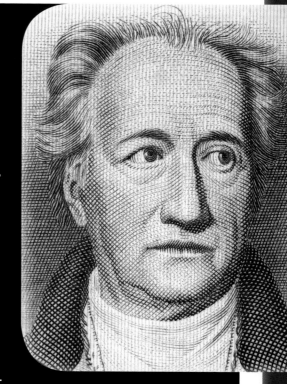

German author Johann Wolfgang von Goethe believed in reincarnation.

Hypnosis has been used successfully to treat a number of disorders, including phobias.

Another patient of Dr. Weiss's, Erin, had always been terrified of someone touching her neck. Through past life regression therapy, Dr. Weiss discovered that Erin was once a prostitute who had died by being strangled. In one vision, she saw a man starting to strangle her as she put on stockings.

Some regression therapies have been harder to explain. One of Dr. Weiss's patients was a female Chinese surgeon who spoke no English at all. But under hypnosis she began speaking fluent English. She said she was in northern California in the 1850s having an argument with her husband.

The Scientific Take: A Coping Mechanism

Are reincarnation stories the products of vivid imaginations? A scientific explanation for reincarnation may be that a person is so desperate to have relief from her fear that she accepts a belief in reincarnation. With this belief firmly rooted, her imagination could create past life scenarios that help her resolve her fears. Jim B. Tucker, an associate psychiatry professor at the University of Virginia Medical Center's Division of Perceptual Studies, said in an article that reincarnation in some form could be scientifically explained. "Quantum physics indicates that our physical world may grow out of our consciousness," Tucker said. "That's a view held not just by me, but by a number of physicists as well."

Reincarnation within a Family

On May 5, 1957, John and Florence Pollock lost their two daughters when a car veered off the road and ran them over. A year after the accident, Florence became pregnant. She gave birth to twins. John was convinced the twins would be the reincarnation of his lost daughters. One of the twins had a scar on her forehead similar to a scar that one of the dead sisters had gotten in a bicycle accident. The family moved when the twins were three months old, but when they were about four, the family drove back through their old town and the girls identified many of the places where the dead sisters once played. The twins even knew the names of a teddy bear and doll that belonged to their departed sisters, although they had never heard the names before. They played a morbid game where one sister put her head on the lap of the other, who would say that blood was coming out of her twin's eyes because a car had struck her.

CHAPTER 4

ZOMBIES

Although the idea of the dead rising has been discussed for millennia, the idea of cannibalistic zombies is very recent. Zombies are nothing more than science fiction.

Zombies have become a modern cultural craze. Zombies are the dead brought back to life, but their bodies are in a constant state of **decomposition**. These formerly normal human beings have become **cannibals** in death. They usually have no other function than to ceaselessly come after living human beings, and then kill them and eat their flesh and brains. In most cases, they do not speak, and the only way zombies can be stopped is by a blow or bullet to the head. They also go by the name of walkers, roamers, lurkers, biters, and the infected.

Scholars have found that the idea of the walking dead dates back to at least the 700s. During that time, some people in Ireland believed that people could rise from the dead. They were called **revenants**. These reanimated corpses would seek revenge on living people who betrayed them. They needed a spark of reanimation, however, to come back to life. To prevent this return to life, it was thought that a large stone might be jammed in the jaws of the deceased to block any spirit from reentering.

The word zombie originated in central Africa from the word *nzambi*, which means "spirit of a dead person." *The Oxford English Dictionary* states that the word *zombie* first appeared in English when historian Robert Southey mentioned it around 1810 in his book *History of Brazil*. Although the concept of zombies dates back even further to the eighth century, zombie lore really developed and thrived as a part of voodoo culture in Haiti in the 17th and 18th centuries. At that time, Haiti

Words to Understand

Cannibal: A human that eats another human's flesh.

Decomposition: The state or process of rotting.

Resurrect: Restore a dead person to life.

Revenant: A person who has returned from the dead.

Bram Stoker was the author of the novel Dracula. His tale was inspired by the historical figure Vlad the Impaler as well as an Irish legend of an evil ruler who had to be killed three times after he returned from the dead, searching for blood to sustain him.

was known as Saint-Domingue and was ruled by France. The French ran sugar plantations there using slaves from Africa who were often treated brutally and died young.

Many slaves believed that they would be free after they died and live peacefully in the afterlife. Those who committed suicide, however, would get no such reward. They were doomed to become the undead and lurk about the plantations for eternity as soulless creatures. Some thought murder victims might suffer the same fate. In time, the lore of the zombie evolved as part of the voodoo religion, which developed a belief that corpses could be brought back to life by priests, shamans, or powerful sorcerers called bokors. They could be controlled to serve as slaves and carry out tasks. Stories spread of entire plantations being worked by zombie slaves, and scholars of voodoo history say that the myth of the zombie arose out of an anxiety over slavery. No evidence was ever found that these zombie work camps existed.

In the 20th century, American movies and comics embraced the lore of the zombie and transformed it again. Certainly, George Romero's 1968 horror film classic *Night of the Living Dead* gave new life to zombies (so to speak). There are variations on how zombieism spreads. It can be from the bite of another zombie or from a virus, radiation, an experiment gone wrong, or black magic. Often, when zombies arise, it's part of an end-of-the-world scenario. In general, though, zombies mean trouble.

A Real Zombie?

On May 2, 1962, Clairvius Narcisse died in Haiti after suffering for weeks with a high fever. He was buried and fondly remembered by his family. In 1980, 18 years later, his sister saw a slow-moving, vacant-eyed man coming toward her. He told the woman that he was Clairvius. A voodoo doctor had **resurrected** him shortly after he died and enslaved him on a sugar plantation. Two hundred members of his family and community swear that Narcisse was resurrected.

The Scientific Take: A Biological Transformation

When Harvard professor Wade Davis heard the story of Clairvius Narcisse, he decided to travel to Haiti to meet with any witch doctors he could find. He encountered Max Beauvoir, who was known as the Pope of Voodoo—he headed a coalition of about 6,000 witch doctors. Max used a magical zombie powder to resurrect the dead. Davis analyzed the powder and found it to contain crushed skull of a deceased baby, freshly killed blue lizards, a dead toad wrapped in a dried sea worm, and an "itching pea," an exotic type of vine. The formula had one additional component: a powerful neurotoxin from the puffer fish called tetrodotoxin, which acts as a nerve poison. When Dr. Davis tested the powder on rats, they became comatose for about six hours and then returned to life. Davis discovered that voodoo doctors may also use a poison-

A voodoo ceremony in Haiti.

ous plant called Jimsonweed, which causes "amnesia, delirium and suggestibility." Once a person was "resurrected," he or she could be given the Jimsonweed and then be easily mind-controlled. Using these biological ingredients a person might become "zombified."

Real-Deal Resurrections

Although there are very few stories of people encountering a real zombie, there are eyewitness accounts of people who "return from the dead." Stories of resurrection go back to the Bible, but in modern times there are cases where someone who was thought to be dead suddenly arises. In the Philippines in 2014, a three-year-old girl was declared dead in a hospital where she had been fighting a severe fever. The attending physician did not detect a pulse or any breathing. The girl was put in a coffin for her funeral. At the funeral, her parents wanted to make sure their daughter was properly arranged. When they lifted the lid, they saw her head move. Her parents were shocked but overjoyed.

In a similar story in Belem in Brazil in 2012, a two-year-old woke up in his coffin at his funeral and asked his dad for a glass of water. Everyone screamed as he came back to life. Unfortunately, in this incident, the boy was truly sick and died shortly after. In Mississippi in 2014, 78-year-old Walter Williams was thought to have died and was put in a body bag. Right before he was about to be embalmed, Walter started kicking inside the bag. Scientific reports in these cases usually find that the pulse and breathing is so faint that they are virtually undetectable.

The most famous resurrection in the Bible is that of Jesus.

CHAPTER 5

SPIRIT COMMUNICATION

The Committee for Skeptical Inquiry explains that when mediums appear to reveal personal information, it is likely educated guesswork.

The concept of communicating with the dead goes back centuries. Ancient Egyptians believed that the dead could communicate with the living and the living could make contact with the deceased. When a person died, his or her energy became an *akh* or transfigured spirit. In her book *Religion and Ritual in Ancient Egypt*, Emily Teeter explains that the akh lived in the world of the dead and the gods but could communicate with the living and help or hinder them.

The Greeks believed that at the moment of death the psyche, or spirit of the dead, left the body. Temples were erected in places thought to be entrances to the Underworld (where the spirits resided). At these temples, the Greeks practiced **necromancy** in order to receive prophecies.

Queen Elizabeth I of England (1533–1603) would gaze into a unique Aztec mirror that supposedly gave her visions of a departed friend. In time, the notion of communicating with the dead became known as *Spiritualism*. Some believe those who die become angels and angels communicate with us on earth. Many of the Christian faith and other religions believe that you cannot and should not communicate with the dead.

Mediums Reach Beyond the Grave

During the mid-1800s, the idea of *mediumship* rose as part of the Spiritualist Movement in America.

Words to Understand

Automatic writing: Writing said to come from a spiritual, occult, or subconscious level rather than from conscious intention.

Channel: To communicate with spiritual entities and allow their messages to flow through a person.

Levitate: To rise in the air by supernatural or magical power.

Necromancy: An ability to summon and control things that are dead.

Spectral: Ghostly.

This was a belief based on supposed communication with the spirits of the dead, especially through mediums—people who supposedly have a unique ability to communicate with those who have died or to channel their spirits through their bodies. By the 1840s, the United States was expanding rapidly, and as cities became overcrowded, disease spread. Epidemics of cholera, whooping cough, influenza, and diphtheria killed many. One-third of all infants born in cities did not reach their first birthday. The fact that death affected so many families might explain why Spiritualism thrived at this time.

The movement is said to have begun in 1848 with the Fox sisters of Hydesville, NY. On March 31 of that year, the sisters said they had contacted the spirit of a murdered peddler, whose spirit communicated through rapping sounds. A group of Quakers in upstate New York

A necromancer casts a spell to revive the dead.

embraced the sisters and took them under their wing. A few years later, investigators found that the girls were creating the knocking noises themselves—though believers in spiritualism refused to accept it. Forty years after they began, however, the sisters themselves confessed that all their rappings and supposed connections with the afterlife were phony.

Mediums sometimes tried to reach the dead through dramatic séances. A typical séance consists of a group of people gathered around a table in dim lighting, often candlelight. Participants close their eyes and hold hands. Everyone concentrates on the spirit they wish to summon. Then the medium asks the spirit to join them and offer some sign of his or her presence. Those present may ask questions, usually ones that could be answered with a yes or no. Sometimes the spirit will answer in knocks, or through a Ouija board, or possibly a pendulum (a weighted object at the end of chain that the medium holds up—it may swing north and south for "yes" or east to west for "no"). A spirit might also communicate through "**automatic writing**," whereby the medium writes out messages supposedly coming through from the other side. The medium may also **channel** the spirit, whereby the deceased takes over the medium's body and answers questions through him or her.

Mary Todd Lincoln, the wife of President Lincoln, held séances in the White House to try to communicate with their son William, who had died at age 11 from typhoid fever. One famous medium in the 1800s, Daniel Dunglas Home, was most remarkably known for his ability to **levitate** during séances. His sessions also included **spectral** lights, rappings, and ghostly hands that reportedly appeared and actually shook hands with séance participants. In one séance, witnesses said he went into a trance and actually floated out a third story window and back in another window. Because he performed in bright light, no fraud could be detected.

Interest in mediums waned somewhat at the turn of the 19th century but regained popularity during and after World War I when many lost loved ones in battle. Arthur Conan Doyle, the creator of Sherlock Holmes, wrote more than 60 books on Spiritualism. He was convinced the magician and escape artist Houdini had supernatural powers, but Houdini would not be

When people want to communicate with the dead, they may participate in a séance.

converted. Although Houdini famously said séances were nothing but fakery, he told his wife that just in case, when he died, she should try to contact him. Houdini died on October 31, 1926, and every year people hold séances to try to contact his spirit.

The Scientific Take: It Comes from Within

Most scientists have deemed spirit communication as trickery. The Committee for Skeptical Inquiry explains that mediums reporting supposedly personal information that only the person could know likely comes down to educated guesswork. The "psychic" obtains clues by observing dress and body language (noting expressions that indicate when one is on or off track), asking questions (which if correct will appear as "hits" but otherwise will seem like innocent queries), and inviting the subject to interpret the vague statements offered. When it comes to channeling, James Alcock, a professor at York University in Canada, wrote that people may be using a mental process called automatism. With automatism, the person clears his or her mind and then lets random images, thoughts, and symbols enter. He or she then tells what appears in the mind as if it were messages from the dead.

A Modern Medium

American author and psychic medium John Edward is one of a handful of living mediums whose apparent uncanny ability is difficult to disprove. Even as a young boy he would tell his parents family stories that occurred before he was born. He saw strange auras around his teachers. Edward believes that we all have a soul, and after we die, our energy still exists. He also believes that loved ones sometimes watch over us and offer advice. He feels like he's being impressed with energy when he delivers messages from those who have passed, giving details that only the loved ones know. At one event, he sensed someone in the audience had lost a son and related that the boy liked to be called by his last name. When he did a "reading" with one woman who had lost her husband in a car accident, Edward saw a bell. The man had given his wife a souvenir bell before he left on the business trip during which he died. For another person, he picked up on signals that a family member had been shot in an accident, which he had.

The Ouija Board

Pronounced *wee-je* or *wee-gee*, this wooden board printed with letters and "yes" and "no" in opposite corners appeared on the market in the early 1890s. "The Wonderful Talking Board" was sold as a novelty or toy that could mysteriously answer questions about the past, present, and future. To communicate with the mysterious realm that held all these answers, people had to sit around the board and place their fingertips lightly on a tear-shaped device called a planchette. Users would ask the Ouija board a question and the planchette would move to letters to spell out answers or reply with yes or no.

In 1890, Charles Kennard of Baltimore, MD, seized on this interest in Spiritualism (communicating with the dead) and began producing the boards for sale to the general public. At first, he and his collaborators did not have a name for the board; so they asked the board what it should be called. As the story goes, the board itself told them to name it "Ouija." They asked the board what that meant. It replied: "Good luck."

How does science explain motions from the Ouija board? It may be due to something called

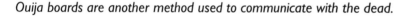

Ouija boards are another method used to communicate with the dead.

A Few Eerie Ouija Tales

• In Italy in 1978, University of Bologna professors gathered with a Ouija board to find a kidnapped politician. The board spelled out "Gradoli." Unfortunately, the criminals killed the politician, but he was found to be in a house on a street named Via Gradoli.

• In 1920, many people in the town of El Cerrito, CA, went mad, ripping off their clothes after using a Ouija board. Town officials banned the board.

• According to one board-user's tale reported online in 2014, a group was playing with the Ouija board when they got creeped out by a porcelain doll in the room. They put the doll in another room face down in a pile of towels. When they returned to the Ouija board, it spelled out "D-O-L-L." They opened the door and the doll was standing at the entranceway staring at them.

the *ideomotor* effect, whereby a person is making motions unconsciously. With the Ouija board, a small almost imperceivable muscular movement could be causing the planchette to move.

The Ouija board, which continues to be sold today, was a huge hit and has remained a steady seller for decades. Sales often went up during times of stress—such as World War I and during the 1960s as millions of American troops were shipped out to fight the war in Vietnam. For most of its existence, the board was generally considered harmless fun, but after the film *The Exorcist* hit theaters in the early 1970s, the board was increasingly viewed as a tool for dark forces. Religious leaders denounced it, and its popularity decreased for a time. But interest in the board has seen an uptick in recent years. The popular movie *Paranormal Activity* featured the Ouija and it has shown up on TV shows such as *Breaking Bad* and *Castle*. You can now find the Ouija board image printed on mouse pads, T-shirts, underwear, and beyond.

A critical historical look at 19th-centry spiritualism and seances.

Series Glossary

Affliction: Something that causes pain or suffering.

Afterlife: Life after death.

Anthropologist: A professional who studies the origin, development, and behavioral aspects of human beings and their societies, especially primitive societies.

Apparition: A ghost or ghostlike image of a person.

Archaeologist: A person who studies human history and prehistory through the excavation of sites and the analysis of artifacts and other physical remains found.

Automaton: A person who acts in a mechanical, machinelike way as if in trance.

Bipolar disorder: A mental condition marked by alternating periods of elation and depression.

Catatonic: To be in a daze or stupor.

Celestial: Relating to the sky or heavens.

Charlatan: A fraud.

Chronic: Continuing for a long time; used to describe an illness or medical condition generally lasting longer than three months.

Clairvoyant: A person who claims to have a supernatural ability to perceive events in the future or beyond normal sensory contact.

Cognition: The mental action or process of acquiring knowledge and understanding through thought, experience, and the senses.

Déjà vu: A sensation of experiencing something that has happened before when experienced for the first time.

Delirium: A disturbed state of mind characterized by confusion, disordered speech, and hallucinations.

Dementia: A chronic mental condition caused by brain disease or injury and characterized by memory disorders, personality changes, and impaired reasoning.

Dissociative: Related to a breakdown of mental function that normally operates smoothly, such as memory and consciousness. Dissociative identity disorder is a mental Trauma: A deeply distressing or disturbing experience.

Divine: Relating to God or a god.

Ecstatic: A person subject to mystical experiences.

Elation: Great happiness.

Electroencephalogram (EEG): A test that measures and records the electrical activity of the brain.

Endorphins: Hormones secreted within the brain and nervous system that trigger a positive feeling in the body.

ESP (extrasensory perception): An ability to communicate or understand outside of normal sensory capability, such as in telepathy and clairvoyance.

Euphoria: An intense state of happiness; elation.

Hallucinate: To experience a perception of something that seems real but is not actually present.

Immortal: Living forever.

Inhibition: A feeling that makes one self-conscious and unable to act in a relaxed and natural way.

Involuntary: Not subject to a person's control.

Karma: A Buddhist belief that whatever one does comes back—a person's actions can determine his or her reincarnation.

Levitate: To rise in the air by supernatural or magical power.

Malevolent: Evil.

Malignant: Likely to grow and spread in a fast and uncontrolled way that can cause death.

Mayhem: Chaos.

Mesmerize: To hold someone's attention so that he or she notices nothing else.

Mindfulness: A meditation practice for bringing one's attention to the internal and external experiences occurring in the present moment.

Monolith: A giant, single upright block of stone, especially as a monument.

Motivational: Designed to promote a willingness to do or achieve something.

Motor functions: Muscle and nerve acts that produce motion. Fine motor functions include writing and tying shoes; gross motor functions are large movements such as walking and kicking.

Mystics: People who have supernatural knowledge or experiences; they have a supposed insight into spirituality and mysteries transcending ordinary human knowledge.

Necromancy: An ability to summon and control things that are dead.

Neurological: Related to the nervous system or neurology (a branch of medicine concerning diseases and disorders of the nervous system).

Neuroplasticity: The ability of the brain to form and reorganize synaptic connections, especially in response to learning or experience, or following injury.

Neuroscientist: One who studies the nervous system

Neurotransmitters: Chemicals released by nerve fibers that transmit signals across a synapse (the gap between nerve cells).

Occult: Of or relating to secret knowledge of supernatural things.

Olfactory: Relating to the sense of smell.

Out-of-body experience: A sensation of being outside one's body, floating above and observing events, often when unconscious or clinically dead.

Papyrus: A material prepared in ancient Egypt from the pithy stem of a water plant, used to make sheets for writing or painting on, rope, sandals, and boats.

Paralysis: An inability to move or act.

Paranoid: Related to a mental condition involving intense anxious or fearful feelings and thoughts often related to persecution, threat, or conspiracy.

Paranormal: Beyond the realm of the normal; outside of commonplace scientific understanding.

Paraphysical: Not part of the physical word; often used in relation to supernatural occurrences.

Parapsychologist: A person who studies paranormal and psychic phenomena.

Parapsychology: Study of paranormal and psychic phenomena considered inexplicable in the world of traditional psychology.

Phobia: Extreme irrational fear.

Physiologist: A person who studies the workings of living systems.

Precognition: Foreknowledge of an event through some sort of ESP.

Premonition: A strong feeling that something is about to happen, especially something unpleasant.

Pseudoscience: Beliefs or practices that may appear scientific, but have not been proven by any scientific method.

Psychiatric: Related to mental illness or its treatment.

Psychic: Of or relating to the mind; often used to describe mental powers that science cannot explain.

Psychokinesis: The ability to move or manipulate objects using the mind alone.

Psychological: Related to the mental and emotional state of a person.

PTSD: Post-traumatic stress disorder is a mental health condition triggered by a terrifying event.

Repository: A place, receptacle, or structure where things are stored.

Resilient: Able to withstand or recover quickly from difficult conditions.

Resonate: To affect or appeal to someone in a personal or emotional way.

Schizophrenia: A severe mental disorder characterized by an abnormal grasp of reality; symptoms can include hallucinations and delusions.

Skeptic: A person who questions or doubts particular things.

Spectral: Ghostly.

Spiritualism: A religious movement that believes the spirits of the dead can communicate with the living.

Stimulus: Something that causes a reaction.

Subconscious: The part of the mind that we are not aware of but that influences our thoughts, feelings, and behaviors.

Sumerians: An ancient civilization/people (5400–1750 BCE) in the region known as Mesopotamia (modern day Iraq and Kuwait).

Synapse: A junction between two nerve cells.

Synthesize: To combine a number of things into a coherent whole.

Telekinesis: Another term for psychokinesis. The ability to move or manipulate objects using the mind alone.

Telepathy: Communication between people using the mind alone and none of the five senses.

Uncanny: Strange or mysterious.

Further Resources

Websites

American Association of Paranormal Investigators: *www.ghostpi.com/*
A non-profit paranormal assembly devoted to research and documentation of paranormal phenomena.
American Paranormal Research Association: *www.apraparanormal.com/*
A scientific paranormal research team put together to investigate paranormal activity at historical locations.
The Committee for Skeptical Inquiry: *www.csicop.org*
This group promotes scientific inquiry, critical investigation, and the use of reason in examining controversial and extraordinary claims of the paranormal.

Movies

Here are a few movies that feature life after death as a theme:
The Amityville Horror
The fictionalized account of the famous haunted house.
Cloud Atlas
A sci-fi drama in which Tom Hanks and Halle Berry take on new skins as they reincarnate from civilization to civilization.
The Serpent and the Rainbow
Horror film director Wes Craven's portrayal of an anthropologist who goes to Haiti after hearing rumors about a drug used by black magic practitioners to turn people into zombies.
Unmistaken Child
A documentary about a Tibetan monk's search for the reincarnation of his beloved teacher, the world-renowned lama.

Further Reading

Belanger, Jeff. *Communicating with the Dead: Reach Beyond the Grave*. Wayne, NJ: Career Press, 2008.
Clarke, Rodger. *Ghosts: A Natural History: 500 Years of Searching for Proof*. Farmington Hills, MI: Thorndike Press/Gale Cengage Learning, 2015.
Davis, Wade. *The Serpent and the Rainbow: A Harvard Scientist's Astonishing Journey into the Secret Societies of Haitian Voodoo, Zombis, and Magic*. New York City: Touchstone, 1997.
De Long, Douglas. *Past Lives for Beginners: A Guide to Reincarnation & Techniques to Improve Your Present Life*. Woodbury, MN: Llewyn Publications, 2013.
Deyoe, Aaron. Biggest, Baddest Book of Ghosts. Minneapolis, MN: Abdo Publishing, 2015.
Edward, John. *Infinite Quest: Develop Your Psychic Intuition to Take Charge of Your Life*. New York: Sterling Ethos, 2010.
Greyson, Bruce. *The Near-Death Experience*. Springfield, IL: Charles C. Thomas, 1984.
Rogo, D. Scott. *The Search for Yesterday: A Critical Examination of the Evidence for Reincarnation*. San Antonio, TX: Anomalist Books, 1985.
Swain, Frank. *How to Make a Zombie: The Real Life (and Death) Science of Reanimation and Mind Control*. London: Oneworld Publications, 2013.
Webb, Stuart. *Ghosts*. New York: Rosen Publishing Group, 2013.

About the Author

Don Rauf has written more than 30 nonfiction books, including *Killer Lipstick and Other Spy Gadgets, Simple Rules for Card Games, Psychology of Serial Killers: Historical Serial Killers, The French and Indian War, The Rise and Fall of the Ottoman Empire,* and *George Washington's Farewell Address*. He has contributed to the books *Weird Canada* and *American Inventions*. He lives in Seattle with his wife, Monique, and son, Leo.

Index